JUNIOR BIOGRAPHIES

Portia Summers

KATE MIDDLETON
DUCHESS OF CAMBRIDGE

Enslow Publishing
101 W. 23rd Street
Suite 240
New York, NY 10011
USA

enslow.com

WORDS TO KNOW

boarding school—A school where students live.

charity—A group that helps people in need.

dormitory—A building at school where students live.

heir—A person who will inherit something.

honorary—Given to someone as an honor.

icon—A person who represents something important.

sapphire—A blue jewel.

veteran—A person who used to serve in the military.

CONTENTS

Catherine Elizabeth,
Duchess of Cambridge

CHAPTER 1

A NORMAL CHILDHOOD

Catherine Elizabeth Middleton was born on January 9, 1982, in the town of Reading in Berkshire, England. Both of her parents worked for British Airways. Her father, Michael, managed flights and her mother, Carol, was a flight attendant. In 1983, Kate's sister Philippa ("Pippa") was born, and her younger brother James was born in 1987. When she was two years old, Kate's family moved to Amman, Jordan, for her father's job. They moved back to England two years later.

LIFE IN ENGLAND

After they returned to England, the Middletons started their own business called Party Pieces. They sold

Kate Says:

"By far the best dressing up outfit I ever had was a wonderful pair of clown dungarees, which my Granny made."

party supplies and decorations through the mail. They made a lot of money, but Kate's life was still very normal. Her family didn't spend lots of time with famous people. They didn't go to fancy parties.

Kate with her younger sister, Pippa, and their father in Jordan.

Kate went to private school for elementary, middle, and high school. Even though she went to excellent schools, her life wasn't always easy. At age fourteen, Kate left her all-girls **boarding school**, called Downe House, because she was being bullied. She was also bullied at her next school. But Kate worked through her troubles, making good grades and getting

Kate loves to bake. She is a big fan of the *Great British Bake Off* and often copies the recipes at home!

into one of the top universities in the country. She loved art, fashion, and history, and she hoped to find a job doing what she loved.

In 2001, Kate began studying art history at the University of St. Andrews in Scotland. This was where her life totally changed. The normal girl from Berkshire was soon going to be known around the world.

Young Kate stands with her Brownie troop in 1990. She is in the back row, center.

CHAPTER 2
A REAL-LIFE FAIRY TALE

While she was in college, Kate met one of the country's most famous young men: Prince William Windsor of Wales. Prince William is second in line for the throne of England. This means that someday he will be the king of the United Kingdom.

FRIENDS FIRST

At school, Kate moved into a dormitory with her classmates. Prince William also lived in the same building. The two had several classes together, and they soon became friends. They shared meals and studied together, but they did not date right away. Kate had a boyfriend, and Prince William was busy studying hard.

Kate Says:

"It did take a bit of time for us to get to know each other, but we did become very close friends from quite early on."

Kate at St. Andrews in 2005

ROYAL ROMANCE

After Kate broke up with her boyfriend in 2002, she and some friends moved in to an apartment close to school. Prince William was one of those friends. Kate and the prince fell in love. They agreed to keep their relationship secret, since many people like to gossip about the prince. The two never sat together at dinner parties or held hands when they went out. But

William and Kate at St. Andrews graduation in 2005

Kate received an honors degree in art history from the University of St. Andrews in 2005.

in 2004, Kate was spotted on a royal family ski trip. Soon everyone knew that she was dating the future king. Their fairy-tale romance was the talk of the country before Kate even finished college.

A PRIVATE LIFE IN PUBLIC

In 2006, Kate was given her own security guards. Rumors began that she was soon going to be a princess. But then Prince William left England to serve in the British military, leaving Kate on her own. She got a job as a buyer for an expensive clothing company. At this time, reporters

Kate on a ski trip with the royal family

Everywhere Kate went, photographers tried to get pictures of her.

were quite cruel to Kate, calling her "Waity Katie." The name meant that she was just waiting for Prince William to return, as if she had no life of her own. This was very difficult for Kate, who had been raised to work hard and aim high in life.

In 2007, Kate and William said that they had broken up. But they were still sometimes seen together. Rumors spread that the two were secretly dating. Both Kate and William denied this, but many people believed the couple were still together.

CHAPTER 3
THE DUCHESS OF CAMBRIDGE

In 2010, the royal family announced that Kate and Prince William were going to be married. The Prince proposed to Kate while the two were on holiday in Kenya. He gave her his mother's sapphire engagement ring.

A ROYAL WEDDING

On April 29, 2011, Kate Middleton married Prince William at Westminster Abbey in London. More

Kate and William pose for pictures in 2010, shortly after they were engaged to be married.

Kate and William stand with members of the royal family on their wedding day.

than 300 million people from around the world watched the royal wedding on television. Crowds gathered in the streets of London, hoping to see the couple.

Prince William's royal family, including his father, Prince Charles, his brother, Prince Harry, and his grandmother, Queen Elizabeth, all attended the wedding. After the ceremony, the family greeted the public from a balcony of Buckingham Palace.

The wedding was the event of the decade. People were very interested in Kate's wedding gown. She had always been known for her fashion choices, just like William's mother, Princess Diana. Kate would now be known as a princess and a style icon.

AN HEIR AND A SPARE

In December 2012, Kate was admitted to the hospital. Many people guessed that she might be pregnant. A month later, the royal family said that Kate was

Kate's full title is *Her Royal Highness* Princess William Arthur Philip Louis, Duchess of Cambridge, Countess of Strathearn, Baroness Carrickfergus.

going to have a baby. On July 22, 2013, Kate gave birth to her first child: a son, Prince George Alexander Louis. Prince George is the third **heir** to the British throne, after his father.

Less than two years later, on May 2, 2015, Kate gave birth to her second child, a daughter: Princess Charlotte Elizabeth Diana. The public loves seeing the young royal family together, and it is very clear that Kate enjoys being a mother.

William and Kate with George and Charlotte on a ski trip in 2016

CHAPTER 4
THE "PEOPLE'S PRINCESS"

There is more to being a princess than dresses, parties, and the royal family. Prince William's mother, Diana, Princess of Wales, was beloved all over the world for her **charity** work. Kate has already shown that she intends to follow in her footsteps.

KATE'S CAUSES

The Duchess of Cambridge has many interests. Some of her charities include working with children in education and health care, **veterans**, the elderly, and of course, art. She supports museums, children's hospitals, and is also involved with scouting. After their wedding, Kate and William began the Royal Foundation of the Duke and

Kate Says:

"Yes, well I really hope I can make a difference, even in the smallest way. I am looking foward to helping as much as I can."

Kate and William speak at an event for World Mental Health Day in 2015.

Kate and William, along with Prince Harry, meet with the Obamas at Kensington Palace in 2016.

Duchess of Cambridge and Prince Harry, which gives aid to many different causes.

Kate travels with her family all over the world talking about children's education and health care. She has met with many world leaders, including Barack and Michelle Obama and Justin Trudeau, the prime minister of Canada.

THE FUTURE QUEEN

Although it is many years away, Kate will probably be the queen of England one day. Until that day comes, Kate wants to concentrate on her charities and her family. She wants to be the best she can be for her people, and she hopes that someday she can help bring about a peaceful world for the next generation.

Royals are often given honorary titles. Some of Kate's include Honorary Canadian Ranger and Honorary Air Commandment of the Air Training Corps.

Timeline

1982—Catherine Elizabeth Middleton is born on January 9.

1984—The Middletons move to Jordan.

1987—After moving back to Berkshire, the Middletons create Party Pieces.

2001—Kate starts college at St. Andrews in Scotland.

2002—Kate and William start dating.

2005—Kate graduates from St. Andrews with honors.

2006—Kate begins working for a clothing company.

2010—Kate and William announce their engagement.

2011—Kate marries William.

2013—Kate gives birth to son, George Louis.

2015—Kate gives birth to daughter, Charlotte Elizabeth Diana.

2016—Kate visits the United States and Canada.

LEARN MORE

BOOKS

Bryan, Dale-Maria. *William and Kate.* Mankato, MN: Child's World, 2012.

Doak, Robin S. *Kate Middleton: Duchess of Cambridge.* New York, NY: Children's Press, 2015.

Miller, Eileen Ridisill. *Kate: The Duchess of Cambridge Paper Dolls.* Mineola, NY: Dover Publications. 2015.

WEBSITES

Project Britain

projectbritain.com/royaltree.htm
Learn about the British Royal Family tree.

Royal Foundation

royalfoundation.com
Learn about Kate and William's charity foundation.

INDEX

Published in 2018 by Enslow Publishing, LLC
101 W. 23rd Street, Suite 240, New York, NY 10011

Library of Congress Cataloguing-in-Publication Data
Names: Summers, Portia, author
Title: Kate Middleton : Duchess of Cambridge / Portia Summers.
Description: New York, NY : Enslow Publishing, [2017] | Series: Junior biographies | Includes bibliographical references and index. | Audience: Grades 3-5.
Identifiers: LCCN 2016057572 | ISBN 9780766086722 (library bound : alk. paper) ISBN 9780766087811 (paperback) | ISBN 9780766087828 (6-pack)
Subjects: LCSH: Catherine, Duchess of Cambridge, 1982- –Juvenile literature. | Princesses—Great Britain—Biography—Juvenile literature.
Classification: LCC DA591.A45 W55815 2017 | DDC 941.086/12092 [B] —dc23
LC record available at https://lccn.loc.gov/2016057572

Printed in the United States of America

To Our Readers: We have done our best to make sure all websites in this book were active and appropriate when we went to press. However, the author and the publisher have no control over and assume no liability for the material available on those websites or on any websites they may link to. Any comments or suggestions can be sent by e-mail to customerservice@enslow.com.

Photo Credits: Cover, pp. 1 Max Mumby/Indigo/Getty Images; p. 4 Ben Pruchnie/Getty Images; pp. 6, 9 Getty Images; p. 7 MAVRIXONLINE.COM/Newscom; p. 10 WireImage/Getty Images; p. 11 Tim Graham Photo Library/Getty Images; p. 12 Mark Cuthbert/UK Press/Getty Images; p. 14 Ben Stansall/AFP/Getty Images; p. 15 James Devaney/FilmMagic/Getty Images; pp. 17, 19 WPA Pool/Getty Images; p. 20 JIM WATSON/AFP/Getty Images; pp. 2, 3, 22, 23, 24 (curves graphic) Alena Kazlouskaya/Shutterstock.com; interior pages (British Flag) blackred/Getty Images.